Nov 2007

To dear Jane,
with much ♡
Gai ...

CW00742277

Capture the Moment

Capture the Moment

Gail Gowers

Hub Editions

Acknowledgement

With grateful thanks for the encouragement
of my family and friends

© Gail Gowers 2007
© Cover photo: David Cotton
   Across the Sahara from Charles de Foucauld's
   Hermitage, Assekrem, Southern Algeria

ISBN 978-1-903746-65-3
HUB HAIKU SERIES

Hub Editions
Longholm East Bank
Wingland
Sutton Bridge Spalding
Lincolnshire PE12 9YS

Haiku are short poems which capture the essence of a moment of heightened awareness. Originally from Japan with formal rules, the modern style is less constrained. This Collection includes both 'traditional' and modern, 'free-form' haiku.

Gail Gowers is a member of the British Haiku Society. Some of her poems have already appeared in the Society's Journals and in *Light*, its 2006 Anthology, as well as in other specialist magazines. *Capture the Moment* is her first collection.

For Susan
my mother

Grey clouds rolling
rain in gusts
silvers the window

Autumn leaves shiver
blackberries glisten
In morning sunlight

In autumn fields
pale morning mist
new mushrooms

Winter
black oaks
parchment sky

Cold winter night
dawn of streetlights
chorus of blackbirds

Sydenham woods in spring
under my boot
an early primrose

Hugging the hill
bone sheared big bellied
hillside sheep

Warm morning sunshine
Wood anemones Uncurl
the spiders web

Summer sunlight
water lilies on the lake
a freebie Monet

White across
the blue of a summer sky
the mark of a plane

Cool summer draught—
swaying in the moonlight
light headed lily

Finnish summer
dark pines and silver birch
blue eyed lakes

Neat suburban garden
in the herbaceous border
blooming plastic bag

Through lace curtain
cow parsley

Sudden summer breeze
flowering broad beans turn
black eyed

Still summer's day
smell of grass cuttings
sweetens bitter coffee

8

Pale Easter morning
sudden sun light on the hill
newborn lamb

On the table
bread and wine
moment of stillness

Beached moonbeams
gulls glowing
shingled shore

Disturbed sea
dark waves roaring
pounded pebbles

Indian summer
a slow ball b o u n c e s
into long shadows

In Dulwich park
autumn comes
and leaves turn

Autumn in the woods
rollerball acorns
crunching underfoot

Motionless pigeon
squirrel and a nut

A branch, a star
through this small window
the mind's eye opens

Wide eyes flower blue
awakening
from afternoon sleep

Glossy bright eyed
turning round
to do or dare

In the park
a sunshine smile
a melted heart

Ruined woman
lost her head
in the park

(Crystal Palace)

Tightening his new tie
silken tigers of the Raj
on a London bus

Two blue eyed boys
forever blond
gaze homewards
out of Africa

New desert glory
Plastic flower drips sand
on to plastic shoes

(Sahara)

Open cupboard door-
the baby doll looks out
forever day dreaming

Yellow eyed God
ogle owl stares out
and unblinks the world

(Horniman Museum)

Lips touching
enfolded in soft shadows

candlelight
flash of eyes and diamonds

out of mind in moonlight
he fingers her glass

Heat of summer
on telephone wires
a line of rooks

Turning the corner unexpectedly
they meet themselves
lovers again

Late afternoon
his long-winded story
marries her shopping list

Fly fixed in amber
the young lovers gaze out
from their faded frame

Age spots the gilded mirror
as she colours her lips
a stranger looks back

His old dressing gown
hanging on the peg
beside her new anorak

In the dusk
the child in me gazes
into my father's sunshine eyes

Picture my roots
in my dead father's face

Late autumn
dusk and a fly
settle on her arm

The scent of my father
carried in his old wallet

Hot city
commuters cool
in beachwear

Musak musak musak
silent cappuccino
takes the f-rappe

(Café Nero)

Classy restaurant
visiting the loo -
a bowl of fag ends

Morning rush hour train
a magazine transports her
to Paris catwalks

Pristine white bath
baby ladybird
washed clean away

Canvas sleeping bag
turning over smiling
red silken lining

Standoffish Mrs Moody
in unfamiliar familiarity
standing with her offspring

(Dulwich)

Bleak winter morning
in the picture gallery
Titus and I eye to eye

(Dulwich)

Bookshelves in the hall
spine on spine on spine
a mind's anatomy

Another can't-remember word
mother overshadows me

Small girl at the window
across the village green
father soldiers home

Frail fingers fumble
a paper hanky
now a bunch of flowers

Outside leaves move
Inside breath moves
I n   o   u   t

Pale mouth open
tulips dead still in the vase
icicle of silence

Small cold feet
whiter than the winding sheet

June's bloom
has gone

Remote control
flipping through the channels
same old death

Leaving the crematorium
carrying the casket
heavy lifetime

Key in the lock
echo of cold hallway
welcome on the mat

Home from the funeral
the doll on her chair
stares into empty space

Dusk falling
red and white flowers
on newly dug earth

Winter approaches
a small green leaf
falls to the ground

Open wardrobe door
faded dresses hang
in shrouds

Trembling hands
frail parchment silk
from fragile tissue

Conamara shawl
my mother's scent remains

Dark holly wreath
deepest winter
on the door

Wintertime
on black earth
a red robin sings